TIME TO WIN AGAIN

52 Takeaways From Team Sports To Ensure Your Business Success

Pete Moore

To request permissions, contact the publisher at pete@integritysq.com

ISBN Hardcover: 978-0-578-32587-3
Library of Congress Control Number: 2021919191
First softcover edition: November 2021

Edited by: David Ganulin
Cover Art & Illustrations by: Mark Gregory Siermaczeski (http://www.crueltyfreecartoons.com)
Layout by: Formatted Books (http://www.formattedbooks.com)
Printed by: Ingram Spark

www.integritysq.com | www.halotalks.com | www.timetowinagain.com

Preface

I started playing sports at age 7. My go-to team sports were tackle football, basketball, soccer and roller hockey (on the high school tennis courts every weekend.) I learned early on that teamwork wins games, strategy fuels success, and intensity and focus makes you a champion. Our teams in high school (and Camp Lokanda!) and then intramural club sports at Emory University and Harvard Business School, were winners. We always won more games than we lost.

If you ask anyone who played organized sports for any length of time, there's this idea of "once an athlete, always an athlete" and that is how many people may define who they are. If you are one of these people, you may appreciate knowing that the derivation of the Greek word **athlete** is "contesting or working to achieve a **prize**" . . . aka, winning. The word **athletics** is derived from the Greek "athlos" (ἄθλος), meaning "contest" or "task."

As the pandemic set in, I spent a lot of time thinking about the similarities between winning teams and successful businesses. As I started teaching our online HALO Academy, (www.halotalks.com/academy) I began digging deeper into the analogies of sports and business. I also caught the incredible *Last Dance* documentary on Michael Jordan which helped solidify the connection between the two. As multiple sports leagues began to return (and as the HALO sector started to open back up toward the end of March 2021,) that sealed it for me and knew I had to get this book out.

With 25 years of experience in investment banking, private equity and strategic consulting, I have had the opportunity to understand and evaluate 1,000+ companies and management teams. The more I see, the easier it is to break down the plays, read the situation, quickly see what needs to happen, what is working, what is declining, and to identify the secrets of daily, weekly, and long-term success.

In essence, seeing what it takes to WIN!

And funny enough, the word **win** comes from: *Won*; *winning*. Meaning, "gain the affection or esteem of" circa 1600. Breadwinner preserves the sense of "toil" in the Old English *winnan*. Old English *winn* **"labor, toil; strife, conflict; profit, gain,"** from the source of win (v.) Modern sense of "a victory in a game or contest" is first attested 1862, from the verb.

So if winning comes from the word winn . . . which is derived from "labor, toil, strife, conflict," we must approach business with the understanding that we are in for a battle, that this will not be easy, and we will need a *team* to win this war we call BUSINESS!

This book is designed to help guide you through a year (aka a "Season.") It's designed to encourage the perspective that business is a 365 day season, that you've already experienced winning and losing by playing (and watching) sports . . . and with some tweaks to your business, strategy and the way in which you manage your team, you'll get more wins.

You are competing in business, not just to live, but to **win**. Remember . . . the game of life and business is to achieve, to win, to contest, to learn from the losses, make adjustments, and enjoy the results of hard work.

Hard work, perseverance, stamina, energy, and teamwork are all integral components of successful athletes and team dynasties.

Acknowledgements

In Memory of Abe Schutz, my grandfather who instilled in me the benefits, exhilaration and learning to WIN in team sports. He was a loyal Miami Dolphins and Miami Hurricanes fan who appreciated grit, hard hits, and hustle. He would not settle for anything less than perfection, as he sat on his La-Z-Boy chair with half a glass of scotch, pinned to his black and white TV in Hallandale, Florida's Sunny Isle's Drive condo.

Special thanks to my team at Integrity Square, the Moore, Schutz, Mautner, Krassek, Zimmerman, Cantor, Mitchell, Roma, Pulliam, Neste', Adler, and Croland families.

Thanks as well to all my past, present, and future HALO Talks guests, Integrity Square clients, investors, and friends.

It's been a wild ride over these past 20+ years (self-inflicted pain from business decisions and macro shocks to the system.) I look forward to continuing it with all of you!

"Wake up to win!"

—P.T.Mo

Foreword

by
Mike Pesca

My friend Peter Moore was not the fastest athlete, nor the strongest. He was not blessed with amazing lung capacity or capable of throwing a 99 mph fastball. But on every team he's ever been on over the past 40 years . . . he's been the hardest worker, the most reliable teammate, and the most natural leader.

On the pages that follow, you are sure to glean important insights, marvel at a few caricatures, and make changes to your workplace and team that will have material gains in your business success. Even so, you may be asking, why get business advice from a high school athlete and star of intramurals when there is no shortage of household-name championship coaches who are eager to whisper advice on the pages of books located in the business section of Amazon?

You know the phenomenon; after the coach wins an NCAA championship he gets a recruiting boost, a cash bonus, and, pretty often, a book deal.

I do think that achieving greatness in a highly competitive field like big time sports requires leadership skills, and I also believe that to some degree those same skills are applicable to other walks of life. But we take the idea too far.

Usually great success in a highly specific realm is because of highly specific talents.

You're more likely to get great wisdom from someone who has achieved *generalized* success in a more *relatable* field. Someone who doesn't have unique skills, or even historic blessings in a rarefied area. Maybe even someone who draws lessons not from the time he played in the NBA, but from the time he played and succeeded on the varsity basketball team in high school, or the intramural squad in college.

Michael Phelps has great insight into swimming, but most of his success is due to living inside a body that is built like a bottle-nose dolphin and inhabiting the headspace of a Navy SEAL. I bet better life advice comes from the squat, not particularly buoyant fellow who barely made varsity but swam his lungs out every meet.

A college coach may tell you he won the National Championship drawing upon business principles or tenets of leadership. Less emphasized is the ability to recruit NBA-ready teenagers as uncompensated apprentices. That certainly is central to their achievements, though not particularly relevant to the demands of entrepreneurial or corporate achievement.

The celebrity-coach business book is premised on the idea that leadership skills can be gleaned by the non-celebrity reader. Therefore it follows that the non-celebrity leader, once in possession of leadership skills, would have insights to pass along to others.

In Pete Moore I find one of the most determined, hard-charging but generous people I've ever known. In this book I think you will find wisdom, knowledge, and inspiration, learned from his playing days and honed in the business world.

Contents

#1   Pay For Talent 12

#2   Man Versus Zone 14

#3   Decode Your Competitors Signals 16

#4   Use Your Time-Outs 18

#5   Focus On Today's Game 20

#6   I Need Action Leaders, Not Thought Leaders (10:1) 22

#7   Weekly Preparation 24

#8   Stretch Together 26

#9   What Your Org Chart Should Look Like 28

#10   If You're The Owner & CEO, What Was Your Record Last Year? 30

#11   What Data Do You Look At Daily? 32

#12   Compensate Your Players To Achieve The Ultimate Goal: The Stanley Cup ... 34

#13   Severance Should Never Be More Than 5 Months & 27 Days 36

#14   What Are You Feeding Your Employees? (Your Athletes!) 38

#15   Too Many Players On The Ice 40

#16   Everything You Do Must Start And End On Time. 42

#17 Do You Treat Clients And Members Like Season Ticket Holders Who Bought A Personal Seat License ("PSL") For $25,000 And Up?..44

#18 If You're The CEO, You Must Own A Clipboard And A Headset 46

#19 Slow Down The Tape 48

#20 Please, Please, Please Simplify Your Business Description!...50

#21 What Do You Really Know About Your Athletes?...54

#22 Give Your Team A Salary Cap 56

#23 Where Do You Source Your Talent From? 58

#24 Value Every Possession...60

#25 Only Hire Two Times A Year, Not Daily, Weekly, And Monthly.................................62

#26 Celebrate Weekly Wins...64

#27 Fire Players With Bad Attitudes. 66

#28 Identify Your Top Players For Next Season Now. 68

#29 Simplify The Playbook..70

#30 Set Up A Special Teams Unit 72

#31 Hold Press Conferences...74

#32 Trust Your Intuition 76

#33 Stay Off The Injured Reserve..78

#34 Everybody Likes A Trophy!..80

#35 Know Your Competitors 82

#36 Be Realistic About Your Batting Average 84

#37 Consider Moving To A New City 86

#38 Stop Multitasking 88

#39 Every Month Is March Madness 90

#40 Spend More On Intelligence 92

#41 Know Your Competitors Top Personnel 94

#42 Make Personnel Changes Quickly 96

#43 Head Coach Is Responsible 98

#44 Open A Dialogue With All Stakeholders 100

#45 Give Employees Authentic Uniforms 102

#46 What Would You Expect Of Yourself As An Owner Or Head Coach? 104

#47 Treat Your Employees Like Professional Athletes 106

#48 No Cash Bonuses. Play To Win... 108

#49 Understand The Game And Your Strategy 110

#50 Do You Have The Best Coaches For Your Position Players? 112

#51 Take The Points 114

#52 Extra Points 116

Why Am I Writing This Book?

I suspect if you picked up this book, you probably played high school or college sports. At least 73% of Americans played a sport in high school. A lot of us view those years as the glory years, winning in high school, college, pro sports, inter-camp games, or intramurals. It's a feeling of exuberance, excitement, emotion, team accomplishment, and physical perseverance. It's a result of hard work, chemistry, a bit of luck, strategic planning, real-time adjustments, making modifications, managing the clock and relying on your teammates.

After 26 years, having graduated from Emory University then Harvard Business School, and devoting 90% of my career to investment banking, advisory assignments, and investing in Health, Active Lifestyle, Outdoors ("HALO™" companies,) I felt the need to write this "playbook" to help take all the good that comes from playing sports and infuse that into what we do on a daily basis.

We are all imperfectly perfect. *Everything* is a work in progress. It is all about continuous improvement. The current season matters.

SEE AND UNDERSTAND THE FIELD THAT YOU'RE PLAYING ON

Pay For Talent

As we watch sports, we quickly realize that as good as the plays are designed, it all comes down to human execution.

We yell at the television, whether it's a professional NFL wide receiver who drops a pass right off their fingertips, or we watch in awe at how dependable franchise players are able to achieve top results in critical situations. Think Jordan, Brady, Manning, Montana, Rapinoe, LT.

Every industry has the best people.

Takeaway: For your business, identify the best talent and overpay them. They're worth 10x what you pay others.

Man Versus Zone

When I was playing varsity basketball back at W. Tresper Clarke High School, I loved playing man versus playing zone. There was always one player in our conference who I was responsible for guarding when we played: Derek Brown, the best player on Long Island. I used to sleep with a picture of him on my bed table 72 hours before each game. (Not kidding!)

I was singularly focused. I knew my assignment. On multiple occasions, I held him to under 10 points a game versus his typical 34 point average. He went on to play at St. John's and put in 21 versus the Indiana Hoosiers in his rookie season.

Takeaway: In business, when you get a big client, D-up! Put your best person against it and then build a team around it. This is a man-to-man obligation. The supporting team reports up to the lead. Playing zone with multiple client touch points over time, leads to losses.

Decode Your Competitors Signals

When I was first shopping for a mattress, if you ever called 1-800-MATTRESS, they would know every model of bedding and the price it was at every competitor in the New York area. I was impressed with their intelligence. When playing defense in flag football, we studied the other team's offense the week prior. We memorized their audibles. We had intelligence.

In the business world, watching your competitors marketing tactics and pricing schemes is a tell. Someone selling paid-in-full memberships in the health club sector means they're short on cash and likely desperate.

Takeaway: Know your competitors, since you're playing against them daily! Know everything about their location, their product, their amenities, their employees, and their strategy. When a prospective client is shopping for your product / service, you need to know your competitors as well as you know your own team and company. Intelligence leads to wins.

Use Your Time-Outs

I've seen hundreds of companies and many times the entrepreneur says, "I'm going to change that, but haven't had the time yet."

Example: A health club chain was having issues with personal training usage. They knew if they went to a monthly recurring revenue model of four sessions per month for an extra $99 a month recurring ("use it or lose it") based on that formula, it would have added at least another $50,000 per month in predictable revenue (versus continuing to simply resell 10 pack sessions.)

The problem was . . . they just refused to *stop* and change the trainer compensation formula, the onboarding process, the billing system, the marketing and get buy-in from everyone in the club.

Takeaway: When something needs to be done . . . *stop!* Take a timeout, clean it up, do it NOW, and you'll reap the rewards. Coaches make adjustments every minute. There's no reason an Executive Team shouldn't operate in a similar fashion. Tweak your processes real-time.

Focus On Today's Game

Entrepreneurs like me are complicated humans. We're not satisfied in our current state. There's always a bigger client, a new software platform, a more innovative product to deploy and an even BIGGER IDEA than the one you're currently executing on. As in sports, you need to show up and be present in each game, each day. There is no tomorrow. There's no looking ahead. There's only the current play, the defensive stand, the shot to block, or the RBI to earn.

You have a finite amount of time and energy every day. All the ideas running through your head? Write them down and then focus on *today's* business game. Make those ideas next season's opportunities. The best coaches have conditioned their players to *focus on the game at hand* and not to look weeks in advance at who they're playing.

Example: Take the famous press conference with Jim Mora, Coach of the Indianapolis Colts. They had just played extremely poorly and, in response to a reporter's inane question about the playoffs, Mora responded rather pointedly. This video is *still* making the rounds! See it here:

https://www.youtube.com/watch?v=NK3Jx2yvtVE

Takeaway: Daily goals. Daily wins. Weekly reset and keep going.

I Need Action Leaders, Not Thought Leaders (10:1)

All industries have visionaries. In sports, you have the offensive and defensive coordinators who come up with all sorts of ideas, schemes, and interesting plays and blitzes: The run-pass option, the pick and roll in basketball, the 1-3-1 full court press. However, simply being drawn out means nothing without execution. And how do these plays become effective? Practice, practice, practice! The average college team does 20 hours of preparation / practice for every one hour game.

Takeaway: You must allocate more time to training, role-playing, and educating your team. If you're onboarding an employee for only one day, expect what you get out of it. (Which probably won't be much!) Practice should happen weekly. Allocate the time to winning. Your employees *are* your professional athletes. Some entrepreneurs make hires without fully considering how they fit into the team. To win at any sport, you need position-skilled players and you also need team players.

Imagine how strong your team would be if you changed the narrative, referred to your team in sports terminology, and gave them a real coach? You refer to Human Resources as Head of Player Personnel. What if everyone wore a uniform with their last name on it? Why does business need to be different from what worked in high school, college, or professional sports? It doesn't.

Invest in your players. Give them every advantage to succeed and *you* will succeed.

Weekly Preparation

Monday mornings should be practice. Not 20 minutes, but 4 hours. No client calls or external meetings. It's 4 hours of focusing on the personnel you have and the team preparation. It's the plan for the week.

By noon, there should be one sentence on the board which is the answer to this question: What successes this week constitutes a Win? Is it number of new members? Number of referrals? Number of success stories? Results of an internal New Promoter Score survey? Completion of a successful event?

Takeaway: Prepare, set the goal, execute, rinse, repeat.

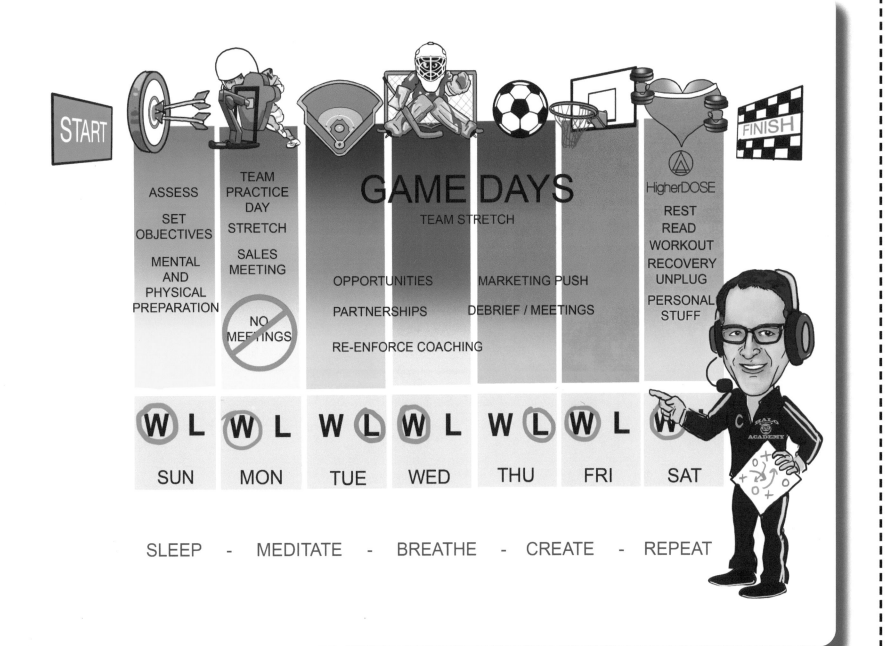

Stretch Together

When we think back to high school sports, a lot of the bonding and building blocks of relationships were developed during stretching. Sounds crazy, but think about it . . . it was 15 minutes before and after each game and practice.

I don't advocate alcohol-centric happy hours anymore, but when your employees are in the office, a group stretch before and after, will benefit your team in ways that will surprise you. They've been doing this in Japan for years.

> *Morning exercise is referred to as "Rajio Taisou" or "Radio Exercise." The radio comes on, employees gather together, and the exercise routine begins. It can be as short as three to four minutes, but the positive effects may continue throughout the day. Just look at the Swedish company, Skanska.*

> *Source: https://ccsbestpractice.org.uk/entries/morning-exercises-for-construction-workers/*

> *They took a note from Japan by encouraging more than 600 construction workers to take part in a ten-minute exercise and stretch workout in the morning. Workers reported feeling a better sense of community and motivation in the morning, and Skanska saw a decrease in the number of soft tissue injuries.*

> *Source: https://www.worksitemed.com/decrease-health-issues-improve-productivity-with-this-japanese-custom/*

Takeaway: Treat your business like a sports team experience. Don't lose what worked. You're older now but the same principles apply. Exercise, community, and discipline wins games.

What Your Org Chart Should Look Like

I used to play goalie in soccer. My singular objective: Make sure we don't lose. The forwards will make sure they score and that we have the opportunity to win.

Shouldn't we think about our company the same way?

Corporate overhead is basically one big group of goalies and defensemen! We make sure the company is financially and legally set up so that we're defending the company and that the playmakers (sales, marketing, and front line staff) can play to win.

Takeaway: A strong defense makes for a formidable offense. That is why--in most sports--the champions each season have the best defenses.

If You're The Owner & CEO, What Was Your Record Last Year?

We love to play Monday morning quarterback. "I would've gone on fourth and two!" "No way I would have gone for two on that extra point!" "Crazy this coach throws the ball in that situation."

We love, love, love to be a critic! However, if you were as critical of *yourself* as you are with your favorite sports team's General Manager or Head Coach . . . you might look more critically at yourself and your business.

Takeaway: Look at your weekly, monthly, quarterly, and annual progress. Be honest about your wins and losses. Don't wait to change your strategy if it isn't working, and seek out a coach for yourself. Or, maybe it's actually time to replace yourself and shift your own role in order to maximize the probability of success.

What Data Do You Look At Daily?

I love watching an NFL game, seeing players run off the field, and head directly to the Microsoft Surface tablet and grab a headset. Just love it! This gives them the ultimate knowledge and data to diagnose what happened sixty seconds ago, learn from it, tweak it, gain intelligence, get better, and make modifications.

In business, we need to be laser-focused on *continuous* improvement. If you're a fitness studio owner: Understand the prospective members, understand their objections, understand and appreciate their goals and achievements. All this (and more) will help drive your daily Net Promoter Score.

Takeaway: Always be open to tweaking everything. Learn and repeat.

Compensate Your Players To Achieve The Ultimate Goal: The Stanley Cup

You want your employees ("players") focused on the company's *overall* success.

Take NHL hockey as an example. You get rewarded for the team's ultimate success by winning the Stanley Cup. There are very few, if any, cash bonuses.

My point is: Pay up on a base salary to build your team, and when the team wins, award them well with stock options or group bonus plans.

Takeaway: Play to win. Not play to play.

Severance Should Never Be More Than 5 Months & 27 Days

I've been involved in negotiations for executive employment agreements for 20 years, and I'm shocked when people get 9, 12, 18 months severance packages to be an executive. I think that's completely ridiculous.

Focus on this sports analogy: In the NFL, the count from the day after the Super Bowl, to the first preseason game, is 5 months and 27 days, and there are only 32 NFL teams in that business! There are over 8,000 companies in the U.S. with more than $5 million in annual revenue . . . way more job opportunities!

So, if you have an employee that's looking to get a severance package for more than 5 months and 27 days, they're probably not that strong of an athlete. They're also probably more concerned about their downside than they are about *your* upside. Don't hire those who are seeking more than 5 months and 27 days severance max.

You want confident, executive athletes, not someone solely focused on a severance package to subsidize their next job search. Obviously, they didn't want to help your team win enough.

What Are You Feeding Your Employees? (Your Athletes!)

With the amount of science we now know about nutrition, the more ridiculous it looks when you walk into a company's lounge and see Oreos, Skittles, potato chips, Mountain Dew, and Coca-Cola. Your employees are athletes. Why are you providing them free poison?

Yes, too much sugar is poison. Let's not debate it, because I'm right! Business performance and preparation is no different than a professional athlete.

Takeaway: Clear out the snacks. Put a certified nutritionist on your Executive Team, and really consider the fuel that you're putting into your athletes, and yourself. Also, if you work in the HALO sector, try to look the part. Invest in yourself. Be fit. Be a physical and mental inspiration.

Too Many Players On The Ice

There are strict rules in sports: Hockey has six on the ice, the NFL has 11 players, the NBA has five starters. Each team has defined positions. Yet in business, we sometimes throw *way* too many people onto a project, a new assignment, or a new client. I found that the best teams are the leanest teams.

Add resources only if or when your players beg for them. Start with one to three (to a maximum of five,) and have *one* defined leader who is responsible for that assignment.

Takeaway: Rarely do you need more than five people to accomplish anything in a well-focused approach.

Everything You Do Must Start And End On Time.

Practices and meetings start on time. Harken back to your days in high school sports or college sports. There's a foundation built on discipline . . . built on respect. It's all mental and it's about accountability to yourself and to your teammates.

Yes, we all are guilty of falling into bouts of moving meetings, texting your colleagues a minute before a video call, pushing things back a day or two and so on, but this becomes a slippery slope.

Takeaway: Being late in sports means you ride the bench, or you get kicked off the team. Your business is a team of athletes, and those athletes are adults. If you hold the line and are consistent with your own actions, they too will comply so long as you consistently continue to set the right tone and agenda.

Do You Treat Clients And Members Like Season Ticket Holders Who Bought A Personal Seat License ("PSL") For $25,000 And Up?

If not, you *need* to. All too often, I hear entrepreneurs bitch about their clients: "They're too demanding, ruthless, always have an issue. They don't get it!"

Timeout!

You signed up for this, then you signed *them* up for it. So fault needs to lie with you if you have a problem with your clients. Put yourself in their seat or in their shoes. They're paying up and they want the value that *you* promised.

That value may be health results, it may be a clean location, it may be fun, it may be entertainment, it may be highly personalized guidance. Whatever it is, the conclusion is to treat your clients and your customers as if they bought a PSL.

Takeaway: Your clients want wins. They are *your* fans. You serve them, they don't serve you.

If You're The CEO, You Must Own A Clipboard And A Headset

You run the team. You make the final decisions. You need to be better, or just as good as your favorite sports team's Head Coach. Fact: A college or pro Head Coach, is more prepared weekly than the average CEO. I have no data to support this, except 26 years of firsthand experience of watching sports and meeting with management teams.

Takeaway: Step up! Be the best coach you can be. Focus on preparation. Buy a headset so anyone could reach you at any time. Give your cell phone out to all of your employees and clients, laminate your playbook, and be prepared to win!

Slow Down The Tape

Every company is constantly pitching for new business, but not enough companies fully diagnose and analyze why they lose a potential client.

In sports, postgame is all about watching the game tape. The Coaches will slow the film, watch it by frame and ask, "What happened on that interception? Did the safety misread the pattern? Was he a step too slow? Did she not cut directly off the pick? Did the goalie come off his or her line too early? Was someone injured and we didn't know about it?"

Takeaway: Reviews lead to improvement, step-by-step. In business . . . slow down the tape, digest what you can learn from a loss, write it down, improve your processes, and pitch (or upgrade) your team!

Please, Please, Please Simplify Your Business Description!

Think back to your favorite team. If someone were to ask what your objectives were, you might say, "We're winners and we take on all challengers. We're here to win a championship. We win with integrity. We are the leaders in our community."

If your business cannot be described in one sentence, you're missing the point. If you're a health club, you should be able to say something as simple as, "We help our members achieve their goals." If you're a beauty products company? Something like, "We help people feel and look better" may be appropriate.

When describing your business, don't make it complex, and don't lose people with buzzwords like "Artificial Intelligence," SaaS this and SaaS that. Your business description should be easy to say and easy enough for a 10 year old to understand.

WIN THE WORLD SERIES

ANYTHING SHORT OF THAT IS A FAILURE

"The mission of the Pittsburgh Steelers Football Club is to represent Pittsburgh in the National Football League, primarily by winning the Championship of Professional Football."

At Manchester United, our vision is to be the best football club in the world, both on and off the pitch.

MISSION STATEMENTS MATTER

Source-Website from each team

Pittsburgh Steelers

"The mission of the Pittsburgh Steelers Football Club is to represent Pittsburgh in the National Football League, primarily by winning the Championship of Professional Football."

Kansas City Chiefs

"The Kansas City Chiefs are dedicated to bringing the entertainment of professional football to the sports fan in an exciting and affordable way. It is our priority to deliver this entertainment without jeopardizing a high quality experience."

New York Yankees

"The New York Yankees ultimate goal every year is to win the World Series; anything less is a failure."

Manchester

"The Club is built on a vision for sustainability, with an academy structure designed to support long-term first team success, to engage with the communities in which we reside. Together with our passionate fans and valued network of partners, we are developing Manchester City's future history."

Liverpool

Our Vision - Our ambition is to lead Liverpool to global greatness on and off the pitch while creating a financially sustainable football club that attracts the best talent.

Oakland Raiders

Keep Moving and Believing In Commitment To Excellence.

Dallas Cowboys

"To continue our tradition of offering you the finest Cowboys Fan Experience at an exceptional value with the outstanding professional service you have always expected and deserve! We will work under the influence of Godly values and not sacrifice integrity for success."

Quote

"I say to myself that I never lose, that I only learn.
Because when you lose, you have to make a mistake to lose that game. So you learn from that mistake,
and so you learn [overall].
So losing is the way of winning for yourself."

—Tanitoluwa Adewumi, a 10-year-old in New York,
just became the country's newest national
chess master. (May 11, 2021)

What Do You Really Know About Your Athletes?

Here's the truth: You probably hired too quickly and don't spend enough time getting to know your employees. This takes time, effort, resilience, and listening.

How much should you know? What are their family issues? What goals do they have? What motivates them? What's their favorite activities? What sports do they play? What hobbies do they enjoy? What gives them anxiety? What gives them excitement? What are their physical or mental issues?

Takeaway: If you know some (or all) of these things, you will know how to manage your team far more effectively. Watch Premier League soccer. Each player needs to operate at 100% every game.

Give Your Team A Salary Cap

In way too many companies, there's not enough money allocated to sales and marketing. This is usually due to the evolution of the company. The Founder is the first sales person, and they add infrastructure before adding more sales executives. Then, when you do a pie chart of their salaries, you quickly realize that they've *overweighted* the support and *underweighted* the playmakers. It's lopsided.

Takeaway: Sales is the lifeblood of a company, and you need more allocation towards the front lines. Jeffrey Gitomer says, "Nothing happens until a sale is made!" and he's right! https://www.gitomer.com/keeping-good-salespeople-is-harder-then-finding-them/

If you owned a sports team, you might have a great offensive line and you didn't invest in any wide receivers, playmakers, or position players to get you points. In sports, you need playmakers on offense.

Don't forget to get those for your business.

Where Do You Source Your Talent From?

The sports industry is way, way, way ahead of the business world. Hands down! Soccer teams recruit and scout future stars out of elementary schools across the country, and across the world, for their youth development teams. Baseball scouts go to high school games. Top high school basketball programs scour the known Universe for freshmen transfers!

Many businesses? Yeah . . . not so much. We put out a $199 ad on Craigslist or Indeed expecting to find the next stars for our team!? (We get what we deserve here. . .)

Think about their advantages! They are *proactively* recruiting, you are *reactively* recruiting. If you want the best, go find the top future stars. They're in your local area. They may actually work for your competitor. They may be one of your members and you just don't know them well enough. They could be from a local school, they could be from using a site such as The Athlete Book that we're invested in, where you can find Division I athletes. Recruiting and finding people that are going to be your stars is something you've *got* to work at.

My friend Mirza Baig at Aldrich Capital, a prominent venture capital firm, spends 50% of his time recruiting for talent. How much time do you spend on this essential function?

Value Every Possession

They say this in every sport: Value the ball, value the possession. Keep the clock on your side.

Every client, partner interaction, or conference call . . . think of it as an offensive possession. You have the ball, you're in control and you're marching downfield. You have momentum. What are you doing for your clients this week? What are you trying to accomplish on this exact call? This call . . . what do you want as your takeaway? Just like your play is going to generate a certain amount of yards, or it's going to open someone up for a three-pointer. What are you trying to achieve on this exact call? *Value every possession.*

Are you running your business like you're an offensive coordinator? Are there certain clients that you should approach with a different strategy? Are your employees and your athletes making good decisions during this possession?

Takeaway: Take a few hours, step back, and watch and listen. Imagine you're in the sky box looking down at your team with a headset and a laminate. Are the systems running smoothly? Are you valuing every possession? Are you really playing offense when you have the ball?

Only Hire Two Times A Year, Not Daily, Weekly, And Monthly.

Think back to your athletic days. You spent the first few weeks in tryouts working as hard as you could to make the cut. *Everyone* signed up with the singular goal of making the team and not getting cut.

Once the team was set (except in certain unique circumstances) that was it. That was the team! These are our players. We're not getting any new ones, and we're not getting rid of anybody. If you get hurt, it's next athlete up.

Most companies these days are constantly hiring which takes time away from the team producing wins and remaining focused.

Takeaway: My advice? Hire twice a year. We hire in January to start the season, and then we hire in July to fill the bench if we have growth. But during that period of time from February to June, we're not making any new hires. If we lose somebody, someone else is going to step up because I don't want people recruiting and taking hours of their day interviewing when we already committed in January to devote the resources, time and effort to select the right people.

Once they are selected and join our team--we play, and we play to win. We refill and reload in the middle of the year (if needed,) and we play the rest of the season. You'll be surprised at how others step up and manage to fill any voids.

Celebrate Weekly Wins.

Something happens every week that's meaningful in your company, your organization, your family, the world . . . something happened. In a game, it could be somebody hustles and gets the loose ball and calls timeout. It could be an offensive rebound at a key moment. It could be a gymnast sticking the landing on a sprained ankle.

In your business, look for the team player who picked up a shift last minute, who helped a member achieve their goal, who stayed late to accomplish a task, or who went out of their way to help a client.

Takeaway: Celebrate the little wins that illustrate the company culture, and highlight them for everyone to see because *that's* the culture you're trying to harvest and repeat. That's a win, and we want to win every week! Showcase others who understand how you want the game played.

Fire Players With Bad Attitudes.

I cannot handle athletes who grandstand, have an ego they cannot control, commit unnecessary personal fouls, arrive late, and have public temper tantrums. Not only do I not want them on my team in real life, I find it unacceptable to even have them on my fantasy team. You must not tolerate it, as there's rarely a team that wins a championship with a major toxic force in the locker room.

I don't like the three-strike rule, I like a two-strike rule. Something's addressed, the person is told how we operate here, how that is unacceptable, and if it happens again, that's it. I'm not sure where the three-strike rule came from, except maybe just baseball.

Takeaway: When your gut says the employee needs to go, exit them regardless of their productivity. Trust your gut, check with HR on the way out, and cover yourself legally. There are more qualified replacements than you think. Don't be scared to get rid of an employee that has a bad attitude for the option of replacing them with someone who has a good one.

Identify Your Top Players For Next Season Now.

As the CEO and owner of your business, continuously evaluate talent. Gather this intelligence by listening to what others say they're learning from other teammates. Ask questions like: "Who is helping you? Who is making you better? If it was just you and one other person, who would you want on your team?"

Calibrate that kind of information. Make yourself accessible at all times to your team (especially to your up-and-comers!) so you can get to know them early, build that loyalty and trust, and turn them into future stars you'll enjoy watching progress from the bottom to the top of your organization.

Takeaway: Players want to play for the best coach, and that starts at the recruiting process which is built off of seasons of discipline, systems, success, environment, culture, fans, and attitude.

The growth of your business allows you to promote those athletes that share your vision in their way of doing business and allows you to grow without concern for execution. Leading development creates dynasties.

Simplify The Playbook

Most companies have way too many products and service options. You need to simplify your business. Figure out your top five selling products. Double down on those. Shed your weaker portfolio. If it's a pricing model, cull it down. Simplify the playbook! Simplify your life!

Takeaway: Focus on things that matter and move the needle. Go hard with what's working instead of trying to rehab what's not working. In sports, you have to keep running the ball. You have to control the line. You don't rerun plays that don't deserve to be part of your ongoing playbook.

You should have five main products . . . five main plays. That's how you win championships.

Set Up A Special Teams Unit

You might be laughing now, but why not? Why *not* have one? Why *not* have a random cross section of three to five of your athletes who may--at the end of each quarter--meet, brainstorm and so on, on what continuous improvement looks like.

Takeaway: This team is the team that would be parachuted in for "special situations." I have no idea what those situations are, but why not keep it as an option? Have them meet with the Head Coach and see how it evolves.

Everybody needs a special teams unit. Something good *always* happens on special teams.

Hold Press Conferences

If you run a studio, a health club, a multi-unit chain, a digital media company, a digital marketing video company, you name it . . . your athletes are more vital than ever. Hold monthly Town Hall meetings. Hold monthly (or quarterly) meetings. Do Q&A with a cross section of your employees.

Takeaway: Be transparent, build loyalty, and lead your team. Stay in front. You're running this organization, so don't hide from it!

Trust Your Intuition

Analytics are powerful, but percentages of chance do not become the outright best decision in every situation. Remember, you're the coach!

You call the shots. You have positioned yourself, or someone has anointed you, to the position of the *final* decision maker.

Takeaway: Evaluate, analyze, be fresh, be creative, think, consult, trust your gut and act.

Stay Off The Injured Reserve

Your health and fitness is going to be a major variable of whether you succeed or not. If you're an entrepreneur, you need all the mental and physical energy and space to persevere, to have resilience, to keep the game going. You have to take care of your body, your mind, and your soul. These are priorities. It's noticed by others.

It's aspirational. It shows your work ethic and it'll attract like-minded people who take care of themselves, respect themselves, respect the team loyalty and discipline, a strong work ethic, and are thirsty for winning.

Takeaway: This book is about winning. It's about taking things that we've learned over the years in sports and--instead of reminiscing about them--let's *deploy* them in what we do today because it worked back then and it's going to work now! At the end of the day, you're managing people, and people like to be part of a team.

A team has rules and principles . . . and a team learns how to *win.*

Everybody Likes A Trophy!

Whatever that means for your business and culture, find it and make it happen.

As the leader of an organization with entrepreneur DNA coursing through your blood, it's easy to forget to celebrate the wins because, in your mind, you're already on to the next deal, challenge, client, prospect, or whatever.

And that's understandable. It's the way *we* are wired. But it's critical to understand and appreciate that 99% of people *aren't* . . . especially those working for you. Sure, they may be the next Elon Musk in their own minds and have entrepreneurial dreams of their own down the road, but for now? They're on your team, they're working hard, and they *want* to celebrate the wins.

So for the sake of your own mental pause (which you need, whether you know it or not) and more importantly, your employees who helped you close that deal, definitely trumpet the win.

Do the End Zone Dance.

Takeaway: If it's a small company, make sure everyone knows about it. Even if they weren't directly involved in the deal, it doesn't matter. It instills pride in the company. It's a galvanizing event. If you have a much larger company? That's fine too. Silo the department responsible, and be sure they're recognized and trumpeted accordingly.

Either way . . . spike the ball. Do the dance. It's more important than you know, and it'll help you get further then you could imagine.

Know Your Competitors

I've spent a lot of time watching the History Channel these days and recently saw something on the growth and proliferation of the power tool industry. Each one of the companies talked about (Black and Decker, Dewalt, Milwaukee Tools) was interesting for many reasons, but what really got me thinking was that when one of them came out with a new product, the others would quickly be the first to buy and reverse engineer it . . . to understand how it's built, how to improve on it, and then make incremental changes to better their *own* product.

In today's Information Age, you can find pricing of your competitor's products. You can reverse engineer their cost structure. You can mystery shop. You can learn a great deal about their location and amenities.

Takeaway: You need to spend more time understanding how they're going to market, what their marketing message is, and how they're competing with you. Once you can unravel that and understand their "special sauce," you can focus more on your *own* special sauce . . . and win more.

Be Realistic About Your Batting Average

In the last 25 years, I've spent *a lot* of time with CEO's and salespeople. It's always, "Should've, would've, could've." So be realistic about your batting average. If you're a professional baseball player, you're going to be back in the dugout 7 out of 10 times. 3 out of 10 times you get on base and you're in the Hall of Fame.

Takeaway: Think about all your sales leads and then come up with a *realistic* closing percentage. Think about *maintaining* your current client relationships. Then? Stand up and announce that your batting average is whatever percent and your slugging percentage is whatever percent. *That's* how you should really think about things like this.

You're definitely not going to close every lead, or qualify every prospect.

Be realistic. Step up to the plate, make it happen, and learn to win.

MLB CAREER BATTING AVERAGE LEADERS

TY COBB	.366
ROGERS HORNSBY	.358
SHOELESS JOE JACKSON	.356
ED DELAHANTY	.346
TRIS SPEAKER	.345
BILLY HAMILTON	.344
TED WILLIAMS	.344
DAN BROUTHERS	.342
HARRY HEILMANN	.342
BABE RUTH	.342
PETE BROWNING	.341
WILLIE KEELER	.341
BILL TERRY	.341
GEORGE SISLER	.340
LOU GEHRIG	.340

IF YOU CLOSE 36% OF YOUR DEALS = **W**

Consider Moving To A New City

I was recently talking to the CEO of a company located in a city not well known for its deep bench of technology programmers, coders, and developers. The entrepreneur was trying to figure out what incentives he should put in place to attract new talent.

When a football, baseball, or basketball team doesn't develop a strong fan base, or doesn't have a great relationship with the city they're already in, they move to a new city! There's no reason why you should feel wed to your location if you're not getting wins and results, and aren't able to attract the team you think you need in order to post up a winning season.

Takeaway: Pack your bags! Go to where the talent is, and rebuild your business in the right city.

Stop Multitasking

We spend so much time doing so many things at once! I was staring out my office window the other day and a friend of mine asked, "Hey man! What are you doing?" And I said, "I'm thinking!" I'm spending time thinking about strategy. I'm spending time thinking about how to execute on my next project most efficiently. I'm not *doing* anything.

Please. Stop. Multitasking.

Studies have shown time and again that it's inefficient anyway. When you're on that ZOOM call, be on that ZOOM call. When you're writing that email, be "in" the email. When you're thinking about the best course of action for the next month in your company, focus solely on that. Turn the TV off. Take away all distractions.

Takeaway: View yourself like you're on the free throw line with five seconds left in the game and the only thing that matters is what's in front of you right now. All the tasking can be done sequentially. It doesn't need to be multiplied.

Every Month Is March Madness

I love basketball! I absolutely *love* college basketball specifically. I love single elimination tournaments. When you think about business, realize that every month is March Madness! You're up against competitors that you slug it out with year after year, season after season.

There are new teams being built to try and go after your customer base. There are new venture capital firms that put money into businesses and ideas that are going to affect your ability to continue to win.

When someone sees that you're doing well, they think they can do it better. They think you've identified a market, and now they're coming at you! The way to focus and win in March Madness is to *focus on the game at hand*. Understand your competition. Be prepared. Be ready to win. Have your scripts down. Have your team optimized.

Takeaway: That, my friends, is how March Madness turns into the "Sweet 16," which turns into the Final Four, which turns into your team being the best it can be for this month, this quarter, and this season.

EVERY MONTH IS MARCH MADNESS

Spend More On Intelligence

In the USA, we have access to *so* much information. The Internet, obviously, has been a game changer. Public filings of your competitors also provide a powerful window into not only their stated strategy, but also into their financial forecasts and how they go to market.

Anytime there's an IPO on a business, there's an S1 document which provides all the information you would need to know to make an investment decision. That same document also gives you the same amount of information you would need to know to *compete* properly against this foe!

As you look at franchised businesses, each one is required to annually publish a Franchise Disclosure Document (FDD). This includes things like the unit economics on each one of their franchisees. It will tell you how much money the franchisor is making. It will give you information on their balance sheet and income statement. It will give you a management discussion of results. All this needs to be *devoured* by your team. *This* is what makes you better.

Takeaway: Intelligence makes you stronger. You should view your company and your corporate overhead as having more intelligence than your competitors. The information is out there. Read it. Dissect it. Use it. Optimize your own performance, and make adjustments. That's the way to win!

Know Your Competitors Top Personnel

Imagine you were playing a baseball game, and you had no information on *any* of the top players you were about to play against. You have no scouting report. You have no injury report. It's just nine random players you were playing against.

Now imagine the other team sent scouts to your last five games. They've got video footage. They know which batters have issues with which pitches. They know your lineup has some injuries. You have to ask yourself: How well do you know your top competitors' personnel?

You have a Sales Director. They have a Sales Director. If you're losing market share and they're winning . . . something is going on! Maybe that's someone who should be on your team. Maybe that's something you need to know in order to better compete against this adversary.

Anytime you're going up against another team (company versus company) it comes down to people. It comes down to marketing. It comes down to reference checks. It comes down to product reliability. It comes down to *knowledge*.

Takeaway: The more knowledge you have about who you're selling against (not just product versus product, but person versus person) the better you'll understand your competitors. Pay attention to their team! What schools did they go to? What is their background? How many people do they have on their team? These are some of the things you'll need to know to compete more effectively and win!

Make Personnel Changes Quickly

I love it when you're watching a game and after the first inning, the pitcher's rattled! The Coach comes out to the mound and makes a pitching change right away. Or in a hockey game when it's 3-0 in the first period. The coach makes a change.

Have you ever changed personnel in your business teams in "real time?" Maybe someone's not feeling well, not in a good place this month, or not playing up to their potential. So change them up! Maybe your head of sales shouldn't be your head of sales this quarter? Maybe your head of sales needs to spend some time in operations. Maybe your CFO needs to better understand what's going on on the front lines.

Takeaway: Move people around! Just like on a baseball field, coaches move players to other positions. Doing this makes them understand what it takes to win at the *other* positions and how they can help better support and understand their teammates.

If someone's having a bad day, I want them to understand that they're on a team, and that the team is all about having the next man or woman up! The team is here to win, and if you don't have what it takes that day, week or month . . . we're going to rotate people in and out. It's just like Netflix says: We're running a professional team. We're not running a family.

—Source: https://www.businessinsider.com/management-tip-of-the-day-reed-hastings-2010-6

I want you to think about that. Put the right people, in the right places, at all times.

Head Coach Is Responsible

Whether you're a first-time entrepreneur working out of your apartment or a seasoned executive running a multi-million business, you continuously put in the hard work to push your company forward.

For those who have sat in that seat for any length of time—or for those who hope to someday—the buck stops with you. *Everything* stops with you. And while a bit cliché, there's a tremendous amount of truth in the adages, "Be careful what you wish for, because you just may get it," and, "Experience is what you get when you don't get what you want."

You're going to have investors asking for quarterly updates, you will need to provide financials to your lending sources, you will need to manage all of your stakeholders and clients on this winding road to success.

I love when a Head Coach in the post-game interview OWNS the decisions, takes responsibility for the win-or-loss, and is transparent with the media that anything that happens under his or her team, ultimately is a result of proper preparation, mental toughness (aka limiting mistakes) and ensuring the team was trained to conquer Game Day.

Takeaway: Ensure your professional athletes are poised for the day, week, or month ahead. Ensure they have clear objectives and have been provided the support system to WIN. If the team loses, the Head Coach needs to own the outcome and quickly modify the game plan, the player personnel and the strategy for the next game. The more you own the results, the more loyalty you will garner from your passionate team who is there to take your Mission and turn it into a winning season.

Open A Dialogue With All Stakeholders

Typically the reason why companies fail is not because of management. It's actually because of ownership. The reason why ownership tends not to be on the same page as management, is because of communication, dialogue and understanding of the current condition of the business.

I behoove you to over communicate with your investors and employees. Be transparent with anyone who has a vested interest in your business. If you show empathy, drive, and determination . . . your stakeholders will believe in you. They're going to back you.

Takeaway: Give bad news before good news. You want to be known as someone who is open to constructive criticism, open to winning, and open to dissecting why things are happening. As the CEO, if I can prove that I'm in control of the things I can control, then my stakeholders will support me through the lifecycle of the business.

Give Employees Authentic Uniforms

Over the last 25 years, I've spent a significant amount of time in retail-facing businesses. I've heard the struggles of owners trying to find the best talent, personal trainers, group exercise instructors, etc. The point is, you spend a ton of time and thousands of dollars ramping someone up to be part of the team once you've found them. So *don't* give them a $3.00 plastic name tag! Give them a uniform.

Have their name on it. If it costs you a few dollars for a nice set of shirts with their first and last name on the front or back and it's an authentic uniform, this is what you want! Think about that feeling you had when you were little and you got your first Little League uniform, or basketball jersey, or whatever it was. You immediately felt you were a part of something *important*. You felt a sense of accountability. You felt a sense of responsibility.

Takeaway: A plastic $3.00 pin will not engender the type of loyalty you're looking for. You want employees to feel as if you are investing in them because they are also investing in *you* . . . in *your* vision and in *your* company. So outfit them accordingly and take care of them as if they were professional athletes. Be sure they know that you are going to give them the support and confidence they need to succeed. And quite frankly--while it might sound simple--it all starts with a jersey!

What Would You Expect Of Yourself As An Owner Or Head Coach?

A Monday morning radio talk show after a Sunday afternoon football game is absolutely priceless! I love all the Monday morning quarterbacking . . . all the questions about the plays run and decisions made.

How come we don't take that same level of scrutiny and apply it to ourselves as CEO's, managers, and department heads? We should look back at the last week and ask:

- Did I handle each situation with the same level of precision and judgement that I *demand* from the head coach of my favorite team?

- Did I communicate and prepare my team effectively for the week we had?

- Did I really win more than I lost this week?

- Did I get up early?

- Did I prepare?

- Did I put in the work?

- Did I jump on that ZOOM call 60 seconds before it started?

- Do I look the part?

- Am I ready for prime time?

Takeaway: Think about applying that same level of detail and preparation, that same level of perseverance, courage, and execution that we expect from the teams we pay to see, whose athletes we watch, and whose apparel we wear. Scrutinize yourself as hard as you would scrutinize the owner or head coach of your favorite team.

Treat Your Employees Like Professional Athletes

Every professional athlete has their own locker. They have their own position coaches. They have their own doctors and physical therapists. They get certain things paid for. They have a nutritionist, strength coach, and hypnotist! They have *every resource they need* in order to perform their job at the highest level. Professional sports is about wins and losses.

If we apply this same detail to our employees and actually treat them as professional athletes and understand that the base salary we give them is *to get us to the playoffs*, what would we do differently? How much more would we focus on actual things that would make our employees better?

Takeaway: Those things aren't wellness portals. What it is, is a culture of optimization that will ensure years of success. Treat your employees like athletes. Change the narrative. Expect more from them. Understand that *they* are the players and that they are well prepared to win. You need to program them, optimize them, and support their initiatives to be stronger, better, faster, and instill a psychology of winning as many days of the year as possible.

No Cash Bonuses. Play To Win

Just play to win! I've been involved in hundreds of employee negotiations related to guaranteed cash bonuses, and I'm absolutely uncomfortable with it every time. As an employer, I need to know if we're going to *win*. (Or at least have the best chance of winning with the team I have in place.) I'm not paying an employee a bonus to just *play*, but I'll absolutely be happy to pay a bonus when we *win*.

Take a moment and figure out the cash comp that you're going to deliver to someone right now just to show up at work. Is that enough for them to show up and play to win?

Takeaway: Yes, there are athletes who have individual goals and team goals, and certainly there are dollar amounts associated with hitting each one of those. However, when it comes to a company and a team . . . I want you to set it up where everyone gets a base salary (and maybe a target bonus) but it's not contractually guaranteed.

I want that bonus to be based on winning, and when we do win, I want you to pay people, and I want you to pay them *really* well because they showed up and they played to win! They didn't just show up to play-to-play. We have to align all incentives with what we believe winning looks like.

Understand The Game And Your Strategy

It's critically important for a CEO and a Board Of Directors to define how a company is going to approach whatever game it is they're about to play. A company has a specific offense and a specific defense. They do things a certain way.

For example, if I am Southwest Airlines, I am not in the experience game. I am in the transportation game. I'm going to make it efficient, fast, and hassle free.

If I am IN-N-OUT Burger, I am not trying to give you a variety of food. There's a certain type of food that I serve, and I will not deviate from that.

If I am Planet Fitness, I am here to give you *access* to a health club. I am *not* here to give you personal training, group exercise, child care, or a shake.

If I am Equinox, I'm here to provide you with an experience. I'm here to provide you with results and community.

The pricing around all of these is different. The strategy is different. I might be going after the same market, but a different consumer with a different value proposition.

If I'm playing a football game and my team has a strong offensive line and tough running backs, I'm going to run the ball, not throw the ball, because our strategy tells me, "This is the team we have and this is how we're going to win."

Takeaway: Whatever business you're running, figure out what Key Performance Indicators (KPI's) matter. Figure out what plays result in the most yards. Figure out which strategy is the winning strategy for the team you have, the product you have, and the brand you've built. Understand the game. Understand your strategy, and do not deviate from it unless something in the market changes your point of view and forces you to modify that game plan.

Do You Have The Best Coaches For Your Position Players?

When you review the evolution of coaching in professional and college football, there are now deep layers of coaches at every skill position. The Head Coach has his/her offensive coordinator and defensive coordinator at each side of the ball, but now there are specific coaches who have played and mastered the quarterback position, the running back coach, the offensive line coach. The coaches are in place not to necessarily help "manage" the offense or defense but rather, to optimize player performance—each of whom have their own "special sauce," technique, and footwork.

As the Head Coaches in business, we tend to think of Managers of each department, yet we have not necessarily mastered the art of "coaching specific skills." You may have a Director of Sales, but do you also have a Sales Coach? Is your finance team solely reporting to the CFO or do you have a professional (either full-time or outsourced) to help them master their professional development? There is now a blossoming industry of Life Coaches, Performance Optimizers and other support roles to help get more out of your management team and "professional business athletes."

Takeaway: Investing in continuous improvement, focusing on role specific coaches, weekly education/training sessions, and having job "playbooks" will pay dividends over time and help solidify each individual to perform at their peak.

Take The Points

Way too many times, I've worked with clients who had a deal on the table, and it's about 10-15% lower than what they wanted in a purchase price. What I've learned from sports is that, if you're in the red zone, and you can take the points, kick the field goal! Take the points.

They're hard to get. When you want to sell your business and people want to buy it? Transact. *Figure out a way to get a deal done. Don't walk away from someone that wants to wire you money.*

Takeaway: Yes, it could be you have Aaron Rogers, and it's 4th and 2 . . . but that's a unique situation. But if you own a company and you've built it for five years, for ten years, for twenty years, and someone wants to pay you $40 million and you want 50? Realize that differential isn't going to change your life. The *transaction* is going to change your life. It's *hard* to sell a business. So when you have the opportunity . . . last time . . . *take the points.*

- - -

Thank you for reading (and hopefully enjoying!) the book. We'd appreciate it if you left a review on Amazon if inclined.

Reach us at Integritysq.com, subscribe to our podcast at halotalks.com, and join us in our next HALO Academy session!

2021 IHRSA Olympic HALO Talks Team

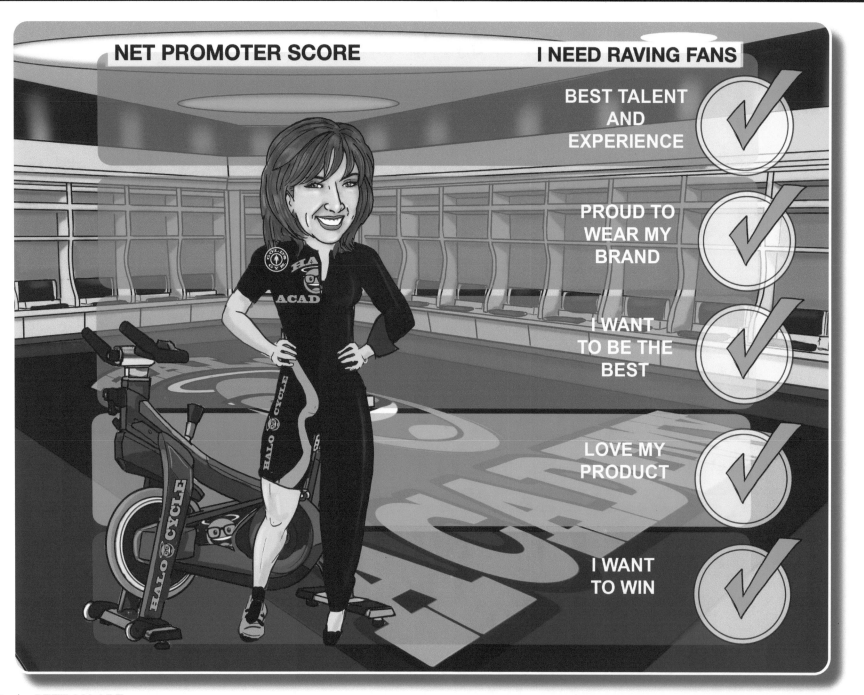

What Your Org Chart Should Look Like

I used to play goalie in soccer. My singular objective: Make sure we don't lose. The forwards will make sure they score and that we have the opportunity to win. Shouldn't we think about our company in the same way?

Corporate is basically one big group of goalies! We make sure the company is financially and legally set up so that we're defending the company and that the playmakers can play to win.

Conclusion: A strong defense makes for a formidable offense.

CPSIA information can be obtained
at www.ICGtesting.com
Printed in the USA
BVHW060048290922
648199BV00002B/2